Rehearsal in Black

PAUL HOOVER is author of seven previous poetry collections including *Totem and Shadow: New & Selected Poems*, *Viridian*, and *The Novel: A Poem*. He is also widely known as the editor of *Postmodern American Poetry: A Norton Anthology* and the literary magazine *New American Writing*. Married to poet and fiction writer Maxine Chernoff, he is Poet-in-Residence at Columbia College Chicago and divides his time between Chicago and the San Francisco area.

Rehearsal in Black

PAUL HOOVER

SALT

PUBLISHED BY SALT PUBLISHING
PO Box 202, Applecross, Western Australia 6153
PO Box 937, Great Wilbraham, Cambridge PDO CB1 5JX United Kingdom

© Paul Hoover, 2001

The right of Paul Hoover to be identified as the
author of this work has been asserted by him in accordance
with Section 77 of the Copyright, Designs and Patents Act 1988.

First published 2001

Printed and bound in the United Kingdom by Lightning Source

Typeset in Swift 9.5 / 13

British Library Cataloguing-in-Publication Data
A catalogue record for this book is available from the British Library
ISBN 1 876857 31 5 paperback

SP

for Maxine

Contents

Acknowledgments

Poems in this collection have appeared in the following publications: *American Poetry Review*: "The Usual," "Objects as Ourselves," and "Rehearsal in Black"; *Triquarterly*: "Gilded Instruments," "Commemorative Gestures," and "Things That Don't Exist"; *Zyzzyva*: "American Sphinx"; *Conjunctions*: "Re(semblance)"; *Volt*: "Surface Gods" and "Oh, Sure!"; *Jacket* (Australia): "Belief and Poetry" and "At the Desiring Vine"; *Montura* (Brazil): "Lights on Bridges"; *The Boston Review*: "American Gestures" and "The Task"; *Rhizome*: "Under Flood"; *Salt* (Australia): "Actual Occasions"; *The World*: "Two Uncertainties"; *Columbia Poetry Review*: "The Tower" and "Circumstance"; *No Roses Review*: "Memory's Sentence"; *River City*: "Logical Objects"; *14 Hills*: "Unforgiven"; *Chicago Review*: "At the Desiring Vine"; *New American Writing*: "Sixteen Jackies"; *The New Republic*: "California"; *Sulfur*: "Volunteer Bodies"; *Stand* (U.K.): "American Gestures"; *Hambone*: "Naima" and "Blue Differentials"; *Fence*: "The Unquiet Eye"; *The Cream City Review*: "Necessary Errand" and "The Task"; *Tinfish*: "The Mezzanine"; *LVNG*: "Necessary Errand"; *Chelsea*: "Belief and Poetry."

"California" and "Two Uncertainties" appeared in *American Diaspora: Poetry of Exile* (University of Iowa Press, 2000). "Two Uncertainties" also appeared on Chicago Transit Authority buses and trains in November and December, 1999, as part of the *Poetry in Motion* program of the Poetry Society of America. "California" was included in *The Best American Poetry* of 1997, ed. James Tate and David Lehman (Scribners, 1997). "The Mezzanine" was published in *A Poem a Day*, ed. Douglas Messerli (Sun & Moon Press, 1997). "Objects as Ourselves" and "The Mezzanine" were published in *Postwar American Poetry: The Mechanics of the Mirage*, ed. Michel Delville and Christine Pagnoulle (University of Liege, Belgium, 2000).

Part One

"If I make a word I make myself into a word."
WILLIAM CARLOS WILLIAMS

Objects as Ourselves

The century's
incandescent. In

syllables of
sand, the

low voice
of history

says *hunger
artist, boogie*

nights, the
boom boom

room's last
good fight.

Tangled on
the ground

like Chinese
lanterns, the

days past
and present;

its face
erased by

words, the
body in

the garden.
Annealed to

bone, brushed
by the

sun, flesh
is architecture,

a white
shadow turning.

Strong as
a god

but sweet
as panic,

the real
is excessive,

its last
bone note

no evidence
of indifference.

I came
here dust

and wound
up distance.

You can
just imagine

the *carne
asada*, mustard

seed fairy,
and *siempre*

mismo la
ventana amarilla.

It's just
as death

had imagined,
an endless

sprawl of
appearance in

black stone
glitter. In

an outlandish
suburb, where

the stench
is jasmine,

a nightingale
sings on

what was
once a

rampart. As
the long

rain falls,
the stem's

transparent, also
the object.

Gilded Instruments

At the hour
of unleashing,

local and
baroque,

earthen angels
cry in stone.

The mouth
writes desire

on the body
in question;

a man is
beaten like

the prophet
of the town.

What verbs
are needed

by devastation's
measure, what

silence thick
as pleasure?

The precipice
is a harvest.

In the strictest
of senses, you

are never *you*
but a cloud

quotation in
a borrowed parlor.

The rigor of
matter, like a

black magic feather,
eats at decorum

and natural history,
remains American

as your old
man. At water's

sharp edge, the
fraught world

bends its vines
and senses,

feeling if it can
the nothing

gather. Down
comes the cold.

Comes of itself
a small persistent

longing. In each
pleasure, the

tensions minded
and what are

years for? You
found and secured

nothing your
own. A white

mouth open.
Indecent as

a sculpture
of fur and bone.

Low against
the sun, on

what was once
a lake, crayfish

appeared out
of small hollows.

The temper
of the light,

fine and ashy,
moves you now.

Lights on Bridges

To be temporary
here, to say
the word weakness

to the blinding
chorus or sink
in counter song

is all the
lovely spending, not
the true story

but what might
follow. Landscape
of the hand.

The body's open
secret reticent as
a plan. Admonished

by her lips
folded over snow
within the pink

town. A matter
of giants drawing
deep blanks, like

what the world
knows—river's bed,
wind in trees.

Life is after
all a permanent
condition and then

the nest falls.
In essence and
in sense, rummaging

through your eyes
for outside things:
the temple and

the bell. You
practice this alone,
in the used

light of day,
on a medieval
screen, on the

red wings of
closure, as rain
in Cleveland settles

on the game.
Flesh in its
stiffness feels like

silk. In motion
and in sound,
the way downstairs

and out into
the brilliance. Pinch-
me-not. Insertions

through slits as
day comes on
thickly. We are

what we aren't.
White noise in
rural distance is

only the highway
hissing for miles—
the cultural debris

masked by land,
dropped magazines and
your own naked

mother standing at
the window. Gardens
are private in

our closed eyes.
A motionless summer
filled with noise

and velvet questions
answered in a
drowse. Red red

wine. The blacktop
shines on such
afternoons. At such

speeds, the turn
of a leaf
may be forgiven.

Re(semblance)

Placing ancient birds
in absent skies,
the midst is

endless. To rise
alone is clear,
the sudden plum

of a mountain,
a reckless cabin
inhabited by ghosts,

its weather rainy
with ash and
bones. Sire of

light. Color and
substance joined like
coasts. In earth's

black dream, objects
take shape as
mind and scum.

The weight of
water pouring on
your head is

one reminder, but
our habit is
confession and the

dirt of history
even in these
photos by Andre

Kertesz of people
reading, the true
light of seeing

in the midst
of squalor, on
balconies and roofs,

even a bug
grazing a page
of Voltaire. A

frocked monk is
reading in a
painting on the

shelf, where a
layer of dust
has fallen on

the pears. How
often nothing happens,
how often it

is shared, and
then toward evening
this feeling of

completion. In its
own carnal grammar,
recurrent entries in

the book of
skin. Normal as
form, every button

shines. To be
entered is all,
breathless and sinking

in the sweat
of love found.
The new place's

old dream darkens
like a world.
This is birth:

the beating and
the drum, eternity
and the parrot,

meaning and the
feeling, chaos and
the boy. Breathless

acts are fragments,
degrees of desire.
None are structure,

all are numb.
The length of
the bridge, its

gesture elegiac, a
string of chinese
lanterns is firm

as direction. We
can still remember
the garden and

its foxes, baby
and its cake.
Are you marked?

A lark in
sauce? There's warmth
in not needing,

but still you
want with ripe
eyes open. It's

like the movie
Wind with its
rhetoric of silence,

where a flag
of a man
struggles toward the

door, only to
discover the recent
day is closed.

On a monochrome
screen, he comes
to resemble darkness

and time, a
meaningless object and
its useless sign.

Circumstance

In place of life's
accumulations

and high slum peaks
the word *hero*

with its pickpockets
pimps
and eavesdropping smolletts

whose features are woven
all over the text
beaten with meaning

One is not strange
who reads these names

essential to the sequence
then as experience

The bookish frauds of nature
complete the seeker's faith

willow weep for me
or Dexter Gordon will

reprovingly

Emergency measures
are what one seeks

and one soft bell. . .

Feeling is seeing
an open landscape

feeble in form
yet powerful as fact

the weary mind
on its horizontal axis

I for example
am not the one supposed—

marks on walls
of the burnished
night dome

The world of examples
is likewise private

mother for instance
writing her books
on her knees in bed

The ideal shakes
but seeing is believing

A small child sings
what the father abandons

lifting the god
of structure
to the dragonfly's eye

A theory may be construed
of names & consternation

It hurts to be stainless
in a muddled world

where staged voices breathe
the sea's aspirations

& all one desires
is a thickened divination
of hieroglyphic fire

We are not familiar
with the anecdotal target
even as it moves

The book is not news
but a place on which to stand
until discussion ceases

I had felt lightly
the freshness of the hour

violence of water
forming into pools

each fall season
a skittering leaf
on driverless highways

imperious wanderings
toward an aperture
in the senses

but nothing this porous
sweetens with presence
or gestures in heaven

an interrupted departure
of scantness and speech

the smoking glass
in an empty room

The world is brief
and pinched in stone

& the fat earth means
to be in excess
of all that is

Volunteer Bodies

Before the first
light, the first
handsome shadow.

Darkness in its
stumble, the skin
you're in before

the next pall.
Bemused by each
sangria, you hum

into the sun
and it all
feels true yet

shines so madly
that one strict
owl stares from

its branch into
history and thinks
that's that. The

century is passing.
In the whiteness
of time, you

can't turn back
and you can't
stand still. The

one world turns,
anointed by breath
and all things

done. The house
of the future
always looks the

same. Bent like
fiction, it's the
past that changes.

As walls close
in and the
last boat goes,

the purest of
lyrics has no
role, or so

love thinks on
her way to
the singing. In

myths and traces,
in shadow and
in fact, the

other world pretends
us. Can I
get a witness?

Naima

Scoured by sound
and the scent
of distance, we

breathe the different
airs song longed
to be. South

of glimpsed, a
stop-watch tune,
dream movie lips

in silk and
space. It moves
me so in

a plain white
shirt wet with
physics of the

down-pouring rain.
Tangent to the
world, spread as

dead, the voices
overheard in
thin Tunisian air.

Dub of ghosts
even with speech
and yet just

song. Tongue's buzz.
Adamant glass. The
third note blown

lifted from its
growl. Language as
skin and the

glass of seeming.
In October light
empty as the

coast, your new
muse stirs, its
old names stitched

in apostrophic smoke.
Like a driver
on ice careening

into control, eyes
wide shut. It's
like they say,

the more you
watch the cat,
the more abstract

it gets sitting
in its bowl.
But no green

wave on a
stark afternoon is
quite taken back.

Raked with dew,
the fugitive world
relapses into fact.

Sweet to be
released in wood
and stone. A

code unknown except
for insistence. The
precipice and the

rift akin to
thinking. Who or
what stands on

name's last ledge,
where the poignant
chorus sways in

bewildered prose?
Freaked with meaning,
maybe ghost knows.

Blue Differentials

As snow fills
up a garden
with blindness and

license, Sonny Blount
plays solo piano
with practiced havoc—

a sun god
with no father.
Against what sound

does the hard
light lean on
fields of the

future? In noise
and in blankness,
you are hearing

a means of
observation broken as
an ocean, unreal

but not untrue.
In the bulwark
of the moment,

the worship of
limit and a
hint of stride

to rue the
very day. Space
is a place,

how else should
we name it?
Beyond melodic, a

love supreme finds
worlds where you
place them with

thin percussive fingers.
The word's dream
changes, a phantom

reminder bending us
sweetly at no
loss of feeling.

On a red
rock desert previous
to belief, structure

suffers from duration,
like John Cage
weighing one note

with nothing. The
pale moon shines
on a stone's

full measure on
the rigid grasses
of Spruce Head

Island. The chill
tone of knowing
fleshed with being.

A sheer cliff's
oblivion or heart's
high wall where

the best mistakes
are made repeatedly
and in number.

Sixteen Jackies

The facts
are dressed

in large
format hats

to keep
love famous

in the
context of

a death.
The paint

always leads
with a

paint can
in its

hand, its
accent never

random nor
its far-

fetched plan,
a deadpan

mass blunted
by a

brush at
the next

exhibition. No
good news

is good
news now.

We watch
with one

eye open
the shapes

in pictures
beguiling and

divine as
a "faux

wit genre."
Many dubious

relics of
the real

world die,
but this

is artifice
dented like

a man.
Where are

we now,
in habit

or in
stance? Each

painting's window
frames money

cleanly. Gifted
with sameness,

the artist
installs an

ordinary flower
in man-

made space.
There is

no impression
worth your

keeping, nothing
you can

say ever
floats away.

We make
a white

shadow around
the ripped

object, which
hardly knows

it's legible
space, but

nothing's out
of place

even in
its throwing—

a wall
of Jackies

in that
famous suit

with its
blood decoration.

Part Two

"An image is a stop the mind makes between two uncertainties."

American Gestures

"Poetry is the memory of language."

JACQUES ROUBAUD

There is one story and one story only,
one luminary clock against the sky.
I remember it was in the bleak December.
I wandered in a forest thoughtlessly,
where love is a word, another kind of open,
and innocence is a weapon.
I think of cinemas, panoramic sleights
black at their centers. They have come along nicely
under the separated leaves of shade,
near the snow, near the sun, in the highest fields,
and then to awake, like a wanderer white.
I wish that I had spoken only of it all
and put a sign up CLOSED to all but me.
I know why the caged bird sings
back in the human mind again,
and thereupon my heart is driven wild
with noise of winds and many rivers.
When it comes, the landscape listens
and we are here as on a darkling plain
fantastic with mythic trophies:
a green thought in a green shade,
a Chippendale in a dominoes etude,
mute, insensate things.
They are all gone into the world of light.
All things within this fading world hath end.
Tell her that wastes her time and me
your mouth opens neat as a cat's. The window square
raises a remote confessing head
rich with entropy; nevertheless, separable, noticeable.
"It was too much," Mike says,
who enticed my father from my mother's bed.
Too late now, I make out in his blue gaze,
in the quite ordinary heat of the day,
a neurotic mixture of self-denial and fear.

[35]

Though it is not yet evening,
the trees are coming into leaf;
the eyes open to a cry of pulleys;
and yesterday's garbage ripens in the hall.
The high meridian of the day is past,
in a different form beyond any meaning.
Clay is the word and clay is the flesh.
Oh, for a bowl of fat Canary,
nature's true riches in sweet beauties showing,
where all's accustomed, ceremonious,
and I left my necktie god knows where.
Then I can write a washing bill in Babylonic cuneiform,
from Marathon to Waterloo, in order categorical.
To wash the spot, to burn the snare
and the full moon, and the white evening star
is pure acceptance, sprouting alike
in broad zones and in narrow zones
like the distant Latin chanting of a train.
Because there is a literal shore, a letter that's blood-red,
draped with material turning white in the sun,
the wounds are terrible; the paint is old.
Then a house disappears and a man in his yard
counts the stars and those of plum-color.
This drizzle that falls now is American rain,
in which the woman I left was sleeping.
Behind closed windows blankening with steam,
the rooms and days we wandered through,
into that dark permanence of ancient forms.
A minute holds them, who have come to go—
the night watchman in a perfume factory,
the old man hammering in a doll shop
whose thoughts are summer lightning.
It is only in isolate flecks that something is given off.
When a kid puts on a wedding dress
in the darkness of a closet,
his beauty defies all kisses, seasons,
and moves with an uncertain violence
among the tentative haunters.
Children, if you dare to think,
in converse with sweet women long since dead,

know that the mind of man creates no ideas.
I think of you as I descend the stair
where the lower and higher have ending,
and I shall stand here like a shadow.
The imagination that we spurned and crave,
a mound of refuse of the sweeping of a street,
shows only when the daylight falls,
but in the flesh it is immortal.
With witness I speak this. But where I say
dark house, by which once more I stand,
I mean a lonely impulse of delight
between Muskogee and Tulsa
and the bamboo that speaks as if weeping:
toco tico tocati, toco tico tocati.
This is the valley's work, the white, the shining,
horseman of the wild party
at the Elk's Club Lounge.
I am slow, thinking in broken images,
but often I am allowed these messages,
like wrinkles on some mad forehead,
the thousand eyelids of the sleeping water.
Under the poinciana, of a noon or afternoon,
where the great pattern dozes,
trinket apotheosis and mollusk.
This is a dead scene forever now.
I am because my little dog knows me.

The Task

We enter other objects more loudly
than a boundary,
speak in the voice of laundry,

which hangs from the sublime
or another line in time—
let's say dissemblance, the fine

tuning of a bone or hope,
when you give such names to "no"
as befits its station. The Pope

elopes with an exclamation,
and love becomes a love infection.
Now structure's in a state of elation.

The others of course are fleeing
into the future, where as a mode of being
nothingness will do by freeing

your outer self from your inner.
The sun still shines there and here,
and in all matters love is the winner.

A fine and subtle darkness settles on
your mind, edgy as a song,
random as description in the long

gust of thought that brought us here.
In syntax as in prayer,
the gods are lonely makers.

He, She, and It define the darkness
with a singular lack of apartness,
a universal smudge where the Loch Ness

Monster can go to disappear,
a hole in the mind where fear
is a sullen theology, nearer

unto Not. The truth of desire
is how it turns to fire
or kinds of effacement higher

than simple erasure. The task
is not a question of asking
what you're after then basking

in its slow arrival like sun
on a ledge. To sing is un-
required yet not undesired: a fun

house ideology. As Ike said to Tina,
"Put some *stank* on it," meaning Tina's
songs needed meat intention. Singing

is a way of casting up your soul
or at least unfolding it. The tolled
bell rings long after sound is old.

Waking into sense or sinking through sleep,
you take your ghost to school, keep
the message distant until it leaps

within. Someone has already spoken
of the "sweetness of the field," language broken
on the edge of meaning. Are you hoping

or knowing? You saw a truck that said,
"therapeutic bread." That was all it said.
So as the camera moves over the red

scenery, the task is already shaking—
an excess of attention flaking
over cold pages, and love is awakened.

At the Desiring Vine

A rolling stone gathers no moss.
Postmodernism disrupts tradition.
He who hesitates always gets lost.
Necessity is the mother of invention.

Postmodernism disrupts traditions
like "half a loaf is better than none"
and "necessity is the mother of invention."
Shadows passing through imagined pavilions

are half a loaf but better than none.
We stage the event in an infinite circle
where the shadows of imagined pavilions
are indelible, mortal, and eternal.

Caught within an infinite circle,
everyone gets a video erection—
indelible, eternal, and immortal.
History lacks mass media protection.

When everyone gets a video erection,
a video condom constructed of lead
provides the needed media protection
from graphic images, living and dead.

A video condom constructed of lead
says: Handsome is as handsome does.
Graphic images, living and dead,
grow in the postmodern video garden.

Handsome is as handsome does, says
Nam June Paik, creating eye candy.
His postmodern video garden grows
until the video cement hardens.

Nam June Paik says that eye candy
joins the elite and popular cultures.
But when the video cement hardens,
poetry's rhetorical factory closes.

The elite and popular cultures
are joined like oil and blue water.
As the rhetorical factory closes,
poetry becomes voice-over narration.

We join like oil and water, but then
where are we? A story to tell but no telling.
Poetry becomes voice-over narration.
We get a movie from the slasher section.

Then where are we? A story to tell
about decaying gracefully, thank you.
The movies in the slasher section
are pure fiction, except in this country.

We're decaying gracefully, thank you,
and shaky as a "trembling prairie."
We're pure fiction in this country,
where a perfect knowledge of grammar

might as well be a trembling prairie.
Playing classical music in a boom car,
we have perfect knowledge of grammar,
no story to tell but a way of telling.

Playing classical music in a boom car,
we drive into the cultural scenery,
no story to tell but a way of telling.
The future is blank, the page is written.

As we drive into the cultural scenery,
the eye is mild, the landscape persuasive.
The future is blank, the page is written.
Necessity is the mother of invention.

Rehearsal in Black

The science of the irrational,
poetry knows what time is feeling
in the language we speak. Casual

as a crow above the pealing
tower, it circles our point of view
with applied indifference. The ceiling

is the limit only in the room;
love is torn between two sheets;
animals eat each other. Truth

is another order, beyond the heat
of sense. The memory of language
is a blind cold wall, a sweet

old man carrying a doll, pages
of silence framed by the chase.
What is love's name in an age

of skin? Everything you face
is just as it happened, minus all
the details. You write a line a day,

whether bad or good, then fall
into a stupor. A line of black cars
arrives at the horizon. In the fall,

you've noticed, the fattest stars
get even fatter. Maybe it's the air,
sodden with nostalgia. We are

what we are, a kind of rare
poison steeped in a kiss. Roots,
reeds, fish, the broken river—

everything is perfectly suited
for a local drowning. Here's a shot
of the water surface, with its mute

tensions and the struggle not
to fold. The world, dispersing,
turns. Here's the face of a god

no one remembers, in the church
of words. The American laugh,
said Jung, is urgent as a thirst.

It bowls you over with its raffish
humor and grabs you by the balls.
You can see the diver's glove, half-

filled with blood, in the halls
of that museum, where nothing
finally matters but stands as tall

as it can. Life is always touching
the edges of a net. Light enters water,
and that is called perspective. Such ends

are met when language and space, neither
quite sufficient, negotiate a realm.
It's cold inside, children have no fathers,

and mothers are desperate to tell
of love. It's a landfill country, strewn
with cast-off things, where stone bells

ring and drowned boats rise. The truth
is confused but strikes for the prize:
the stone floor of the sea, red tooth

of existence, and what the eyes deny.
You descend the stairs to hell, walk
its plazas and parks, and manage to find

a date for the evening. She talks
of her desires, but this is not desire;
it's the tender mercy of a leaf's awkward

falling. At what firm margin, the fires
in the mirror or in your eyes, is love
to be found? Does the sea aspire

to be just water? In the weave of
your intentions, the air plays the air.
Nothing is nothing. In a coven

of mechanics, in the scariest
Hollywood mansion, love is the prize
and a touch of the fever. Rare

as existence, it has seen the mind
change the most desolate landscapes
into quiet rooms. It always finds

the world in absence, doors taped
shut. This is like the movies, a black
room filled with murmurs. As the drapes

are pulled, you see from the back
life's enormous figures falling in
and out of focus, a final slackness

of being we later enjoy enduring.
The story is stained with its own
rehearsal. A handsome bed is burning.

Serious and alluring, a long dial tone
passes for conversation. No one's
there but you, talking into the phone

like a younger father to an older son.

Logical Objects

Like parallel tracks
in different forests,
the world that's all

the case and the world
that won't be pictured.
Toccata in E Minor

is material to the ear,
grasps like prey.
OK, then. A clear view

of words from the room
of the sentence, intensity
of spoons lying in slots—

proposition's objects.
At the very threshold
of sense, we navigate

toward the known:
streets wet with light,
the neon dust of noon.

Emerson called words
"finite organs of
the infinite mind."

Our labor is to make
faint copies bright:
ideas for the eyes.

To suggest, however,
that states are names,
as verbs are choice

of season, brings us
to a text as frozen
as the ground. Thinned

by cold, we read
the winter letters
of strict branches

on a glare of snow.
The legend points
to the actual's hive.

This is called,
in that country,
"a thrust of birds."

2

 In the autumn of,
we feel that even,

locked and open inwards,
in the introduction to,

in a varied syntax,
as if it might,

of similar outlook and,
a curious moral spin,

in as much as,
by the same token,

such riddling is what,
to argue that grammar,

the use of which,
as well as understood,

is usually not read,
not even in truth,

it is this theme,
to judge by results,

nor had they stopped,
only then do we,

to rest entirely on,
no causal nexus which,

as one might assume,
actually used of course,

for better or worse,
of an actual person,

at the world's pleasure,
to deconstruct the eye,

as all are rites,
if for a second,

the slice is cheese,
even in that place,

the name of anything,
it is no longer,

in asking such questions,
what the future holds.

3

Imagination is glass, smeared with light,
opaque at its brightest. But when a hand prints it,
makes itself seen, itself is the subject.
                                For instance,
a handsome former student with a strange red smile
buys a gallon of gas, drives to an empty parking lot
next to Builder's Square (more desolate at midnight,
in the middle of winter, than any grey place),
pours it over herself, and strikes a certain match.
As flames flood the ceiling and rush toward the windows
as if to get away, she holds the steering wheel.
Her destination is the thin calm of absence.
No angels of snow, no "wolves of water,"
only the thickness of burning into a statue of bone.
The gods are simple; they only want our lives.
Nothing is left to chance. Because her husband left
and the children have no faith, her eyes
of absolute speed and all the pressure of being.

4

O, and green.

As to the fairest stars

It always happens again.

Take arms against a mountain.

These are trees.

It wants to edge.

The realm of that hand.

In a sea of rhetorical ease.

Changed in states of avoiding them.

They studied velocity darkly.

Speak again, and smooth.

5

On that page, a chart of the types
of wrenches (socket, pipe, ratchet),
their meaning of course implied:
to twist or sprain, to persuade
in an orderly way, tie down fast.
On yet another, a word that means
expressing determination, the *ifs*,
as ifs, promises and doubts of a real
or imagined future: "We *would* have
been happy, had events been otherwise";
"Thanks for the invitation. It *would*
have been nice." The real and imagined
have with you their say—vestigial
and subjective—how the "true past"
vanishes in the act of conception.
Cerebral as turtles gazing at the sea,
the future is old, doddering toward
the Avenue of the Planets,
with its bolts and arches of steel.
Even the cloned sheep grazing on
factory pasture have the past
in mind: the hot pie on its sill,
Brady Bunch movies, and smoke
from the Civil War drifting over
houses installed now in the present.
Your flag of a hand lies firmly
on the table, unable to change
or conceive of change. Familiar themes
drift through window—the far cry,
snap of a dog, ship in a bottle sinking
with all its hands on deck, the captain's
son passionate as he watches from
the door. We remain officially hopeful.
Details at ten. So when leaves climb
past your window like the sharp edge
of sense, who can doubt the pressure
of desire? Its foundational logic
insists on the chase and kill,

followed by dinner and recreation.
You could howl in the storm. You would
not be heard. It is a pleasure then
to hold a wrench in your hand—the actual
and the word. Something might need
to be tightened as it rushes past
in the flood. We know you're doing
what you can, a step ahead of the mob.

The Tower

Between seeing and being,
the voiced object rises,

a make-believe project
that's barely even an object

in the strict rubric's silence,
an instrumental utopia

empirical as a hook.
We have risen senseless

where monuments mean:
a run-down curve of stone,

landscape as duration.
Glass contains the gaze

in perpendicular zones.
Stacked against a river,

the three functions of pleasure
are structural in nature,

since the act of watching
inside closed space

exaggerates mass, thickens
expectation with an edifice

and a question. One imagines
bells, but hearing is too far

in a slant of stairs that says:
antiquity is revelation. We

eat lunch. In the bordering
distance, mythology takes

its tour. What urban idyll
is this, with its tall strict

patterns sacred as a table?
The sign is in the hand,

panoramic in the head,
from which we see darkness

in the corners of each world.
At the south of being,

people stand like code
in the narrow history

of this infinity's rise.
The diligence of stone

is stern as the mind.
Wind is like an eye

striking the edge of things,
packing them in like candy,

to be themselves and god.
Island remains island.

Time is simple and flagrant.
Useless as desire, written

like a city, the tower is there.
Memory is the base

building toward a glance
and ending on a platform.

A simple infinite derrick
itinerant as the world.

The Unquiet Eye

In the room of words, where to knock is fire,

you enter the subject weather.

Along the horizon, a whiter sky.

In states of undesire, what was thought a crime

unenters from behind.

A mirror smears the wall.

Farther than a flashlight into the grooves of night,

the rare unleaning world.

As evidence and space compete for inattention,

the maid is once again on the point of unsinging.

The shouts of children in their brief unkingdoms

can be heard but not discerned.

A butcher knife "seems."

With its thick ringed handle, it is not less than unerotic.

The century's last death is not uninvolved.

A metaphor arrives wet with tension but departs as freight—

a transparent noun in a haystack town.

The covers of the bed are all unthrown, slain for the cleaning.

Moving through the house like a neutral perfume,

you leave your prints on every startled object.

An ordinary shape displays moral tension

and then, it seems, relief.

As you wander tightly in the same worn circle,

the fourth god's name goes unremembered.

Agitating slightly in a northern direction,

a needle floats with strict attention on the surface of a pond.

Through shaken landscapes, generations pass in unswerving cars.

The Mezzanine

Fumbling in a vein glassy with its transit,
the story will not begin, the story will not die.
Repeating the world like water,
events begin their nervous arrival.
Now we have cognition no nicety can kill.
The mother theory swells along the neuron range.

The social anvil rings. Money as love,
love as greed, greed as a kind of fate.
When the god of dirt's transparent,
the stealthy world's in flood. World of utter words.

In the summer of that idea, passionate excess,
bruised with attention, breaks. Large men
are seen walking, embarrassed by their size.
At the bottom of human nature, something beaten stirs.

Instead of desire, a brown tree and a blue,
marge of snow at the garden verge, and the new dark age.
We sit in the excavation between silence
and white noise, where the blank weight of existence
thickens but will not shine. Except of course
those clouds, stately against the mountain,
which in their brilliance blind grass and shatter water.
We are beneath one now, prepared to be impressive.

Two Uncertainties

"There is eternity to blush in."

DJUNA BARNES

Around the attic bird, the century is silent;
gathers utter ghosts in scattered dust displays.
Afloat in that window, not even a star approaches like a dog.
Nothing is left to desire: rain in open cars,
gasoline fires. History is ending.

We are not, however, among those voices off.
We are the ones in prose whose form
is finally shapeless, except for these constraints.
With the labor of planets turning,
please bind us to a version of ourselves.

The Mirror

When Degas painted those portraits of himself,
"his body saw what his eye projected."
The mirror was hated and loved.
Now Degas throws his gaze into our seeing,
as if we were the mirror in which he is portrayed.

We watch him thinking us.
Beside him, a companion, Evariste de Valerne,
looks shyly at the floor, as if aware of the painter's gaze.
"The circle of seeing shrinks and grows,"
yet for all its paintedness,

what we see is solid as a face
retaining prior sight.
This continues to the gallery's end,
where, at the edge of another room,
we pass the dark narcissus—
dark because we say, minding the eye we paint.

Part Three

"Responsibility is a mode of hearing."

ARKADII DRAGOMOSCHENKO

The Usual

You sit in a hazy northern city
that's accustomed to your strangeness.
You're the vaguest shape in the painting,

yet everything is touched with drama—
this wonderful glass of tap water,
the best you've ever tasted,

birds standing at strict attention
near the ragged edge of a pool.
As foreign memories course through your hand,

you watch people walking to coffee,
still holding their last cappuccinos—
with a shot of hazelnut, please,

heavy on the foam. The season's
about to end. Nothing's extraordinary.
Life's a composition for toy piano—

muted and thin in the hallways of attention.
And then there comes a settling of affairs.
Sunlight shifts; the thought under the music

turns sober as a mouse. With the certainty of a judge,
the usual steps in, its small chin jutting.
Like all plain things, its voice is reflective:

the usual way of dressing, not unusual weather.
What'll you have? The usual.
At ten in the morning, in dust and clamor,

your life has locked pleasantly into place.
The mind does things the body will always remember.
Go on. Sit there with your senses,

in a calm of the usual's making.
Your tragedies are behind you. The clock
strikes so softly, it passes the world's notice.

California

From the cool electric gaze of a Hollywood enigma
to the cormorant eating fish at a Muir Beach tide pool,
the state's a deep oasis of appetite and ease.
The newspaper reports eighty quakes a week,
most of them temblors faint as a star on water.
As whole hands of fog drape over the Golden Gate,
a piano in Oakland moans like a choir.
In the High Sierras, falling snow
is blue as brand-new skin;
the world's weight is measured
by a metaphysical Reno as clean as Disneyland.
Closer to Sacramento, the hum of BMWs
on their way to a software convention
sounds tasteful in the rain.
The motel owner knows the desert speed
of screenplays, since he is writing one
in the neon light of a nude but lucid room.
A postmodern bar just opened down the street.
No dancing, no smoking, no alcohol are allowed.
But you can get a mud bath, scented body wrap,
and whales hysterically singing
directly into your headphones.
The county sheriff has a PhD and surfs the internet.
Relations are wreathed with chaos theory
and the "new world order."
                    As the millennium approaches and nature
politely recedes, everyone thinks good thoughts.
Former cheerleaders join a woman's drumming circle.
The family leaves the Methodist Church
for a sweat lodge in the country. In the absence
of the Soviet Union, Satan makes a comeback
along with angels who look like airline stewards,
cheeks rosy with steroids and purpose.
But they're on leave or out of work.
Narcissus drowns in a tide pool while reflecting
on a starfish; Sisyphus rides a mountain bike
up Mt. Tamalpais, where Zeus confuses omniscience

with his remote control. The future oversleeps.
But in a trailer home in Rancho Cucamonga,
the present has a theory scratched as paradise.
Bruise's star is dark.
          The bargain was to sing, as populations do,
the terrors of pleasure, like holding the gecko's tail
after it has dropped. Disguised by rear-view worlds,
we have taken steps in just that direction.
Glad the puritans came, we wander back repressed
to the land we would unsettle. Darkness
swallows borders. A wilderness shines.

Things That Don't Exist

Things that don't exist shine in the dark,
having little shape but a vague fluorescent aura.
Nobody knows their names. We have to imagine
their thickness—surfaces as thinly painted
as a Lake George window. Eternity blinks
at what isn't. Solemn as pancakes, novel objects
occupy space which itself must be imagined—
a fork, with its three fingers, ancient in the mind.
                    An image is the private life of an object.
In an endless house with no back door,
the universe is ready-made. You can have it all,
but only with your tongue in cheek, the rest in plaster.
                    Original objects are all in hiding,
for which we must be grateful.
When they emerge, as real as bruised fruit,
we will have to convey their meaning—
as snow falls and moisture rises,
as the streets are wet with sunlight
beside a vivid ocean, as the window
is never transparent, as a knot of glass
within us makes the rule the rule,
as we construct our human wishes
from days of cold sun, vertigos of rice,
and a guttering star.
                    Desire longs for imperfection.
It wears in its hair. But we who turn in darkness
gaze in exaltation at what might have existed—
leafless, rootless, and branchless—
each moment sovereign beyond all habit.

Commemorative Gestures

"Then he told me he knew who his brother's killer was,
and that he sometimes saw the man around Kigali."

PHILIP GOUREVITCH, "Letter from Rwanda"

In the town of Nyarubuye, among the million
killed, a young man lies in front of a mission
where his body was left as a sign to others

several months ago. Beneath the outspread arms
of a statuary Christ, photographed at ground level,
his face has shrunken back to bone, so that,

wearing a white tennis sweater with perfect
Oxford stripes, he becomes an aesthetic object
in the planned collision of art and history.

Lipless and eyeless, he reminds children
passing to school or heaven that no place is safe,
all policy horror. Yet somehow this is beauty

in the Christmas *New Yorker* a few pages
from Helmut Newton's portrait of Loulou de la Falaise
wearing a couture ensemble as she hurries

to a meeting, her pinched face hidden.
In her neurotic stride, the aging woman
moves through death toward fashion

on the virtual ground of the lens.
Buried in our senses as in a public place,
we hurriedly turn the page to something

less cruel than sight. The guilty sleep
soundly tonight on a nest of broken machetes,
but we, in our condos and lofts, need only watch

the skies for signs of children flying.
The perfect sentence won't change the blood-soaked facts.
Loulou de la Falaise knows the camera is empty:

the photographer pours darkness into his eye.
So it's not just murder that matters.
As the world's grey grass gives birth once more,

I'm also alarmed by the photograph's intentions,
framing that skull in arms of mission plaster;
how empty the park appears as the empty woman passes.

Actual Occasions

"Leibniz. . .fails to make clear how 'confusion' originates."

–A. N. WHITEHEAD

I'm confused about the nature of time,
like how it might be "gained."
It spills like grain from the empty granary;
it smells like apples in an earthen barn;
you taste it in your mouth on the deepest
of days, but it's just a measure,
like counting sheep by the sea.
I'm confused about the doppler effect,
parallax view, and quirks of metaphysics
like whether this is *this.* Under a blond sun,
the world's plaintive cause stands between
two zones: sweet and sour, lucent and blurred.
I'm confused about luck, the "dumb" photograph,
the "well-hung painting" and why cakes fall.
It's no longer clear who loves whom,
nor does the girl playing violin
nude in her parents' bedroom suggest
that sex will happen. No, this is not
the world nor anything like it.
This is negotiation with a word like rapture.
This is a lullaby sung by a proposition.
Against the thought of sand pitted and shadowed,
the law of perspective always saddens
as it barrels toward infinity
through damp weeds, dim cities,
and the melancholy of the new.
Error is blessed for its dubious fires.
Confusion has a double logic
that builds as it burns.
Conspicuous in its absence,
the "primordial mind of God"
is simple as mud but complex as a fact.
Here the given rests, while we,

the meat puppets, subjectify the giver.
"The final court of appeal
is intrinsic reasonableness,"
though never by the dithering gods,
whose caustic fits have a human face.
Is a confused god better than none?
Time will tell. Trembling on its knees,
the abstract century constantly appeals
to the god of certainty, as if
by sheer will it might create
the shape we had always imagined.

Belief and Poetry

After James M. Cain

The rumpled tenor
blinks. The sign
says EAT—blue

neon juice in
a flat black
dark where shadows

shine and hurt.
Maybe you are
there, maybe you

are not, motoring
up from Texas
with underwater thoughts

packed in a
green hatbox. Trees
at the Twin

Oaks Diner shaking
with their passion.
A lake surrounded

by blue curtains.
Bite me, Frank,
she says. As

the road tilts
up, they tumble
down in blood.

The tinfoil hero
dreams flying over
pines. Oh, town

absorbed in shadow,
the blond mad
king is driving

Yellow Cab from
Laguna Beach to
El Cerrito. It

happens every day.
On light-blind
water, surface gods

shatter yet hold
like metaphysics to
old chronologies where

rage can suddenly
matter. The lake
shakes twice but

only slightly spills.
Blood absorbs more
slowly, dulling as

it dries. One's
concept of dimension
suffers challenge then.

The fence tends
limits, breaks linear
circles frozen as

a rope. Something
always happens; someone
nearly tells all

we might have
guessed. Rob Roy's
blood plot defeats

effete evil. Leaves
surmount the wall
restricting other worlds

and fall to
pieces there. Eyes
blue as doll

shoes, she tells
the movie version
but swells, stops,

waits as Frank
kills Nick. A
cut or gully

ferned drops hard
into the dark
like Nick's last

note. Each short
sentence is mildly
elegiac as death's

breezy manner, out
of breath just
now, drives with

both feet toward
endlessness and dinner;
where, after Oakland

falls, she's silent
on the bed,
white lips pregnant.

Story needs such
heat freaked with
murder plans. Overheard

at home: *I'm*
in the death
house now, story's

cousin chained to
truth and sleeping,
linking method and

comprehension in the
syntax of love
letters ever more

remote. This is
called fiction in
mother's night garden

wet with sun.
After Cora dies,
it all goes

blooey. Angels are
heard to weep
every fifth sentence.

Oh, Sure!

From ear to ear, across
the mind's throat,
the intellect of leaning:

an ant tottering,
crushed, your sovereign
childhood, sunlight

and dust, the wheels
of history, a white
whippet sleeping.

As the wind loses
its voices, a theory
of the soundbite

develops into a sentence,
the sentence into
vacant space and

vacant space into
the object of desire.
Disheveled but graceful,

love with its expert hands
paces the floor. How nice
to be a cup of coffee

on a morning like this,
when the sun is raving abroad
like a satisfied god.

You've lived all winter
outside the language,
but here the language is,

nodding its head toward
something called style,
transparent but thick.

What had you imagined?
An opera of the senses?
Muscle in the dark?

The burden is all,
the process accidental.
The cynical side of the title

casts shadows on the flowers
as they bunch in sunlight,
and the other side believes

in a bloody shade of darkness,
where the undersides of leaves
are the color of coal,

and a musk of fungus
breathes out loud.
Esau says, "Oh, sure"

as if he loved knowing
the most uncertain things.
As the moral quicksand

rises, the plot's about
laundry, which seems
so authentic hanging

on its line, but we
can only point with
applied indifference

at the broad walking
sun as seen in that
sheet. Here the light

rises, there the wind
falls, and all you feel
is "excitingly murky,"

like water under flood.
The portrait of a girl
remains fifteen, with

a necklace at its
throat. But the one
portrayed has aged,

smoking cigarettes
at the edge of depiction.
A passing voice pricks

the world with attention:
So's your old (fading).
Esau is Esau Melendez

who sits near the window
as he thinks of sleeping
in the freaking sun.

Memory's Sentence

She gets out her meanings,
practicing in the empty
often benign sun the words

that might be spoken,
never comprehending
her bone of a husband

in a house made of fabric,
breathing whatever she finds,
the sound in the hall swollen,

dust on the dinner
before the world changes,
moaning and drowning

on each state occasion,
the small bones snapping
—songbirds, sportcoats,

all the fashion disasters—
so she watches him stare,
fully dressed, shoe in hand,

then smile into his own face
by means of that there,
only the past optimistic

because it's undefeated,
a little dog that frightens,
whereupon she turns

like money in the room
to gaps concealing a man
and now they eat lilies,

a plainclothes heart
on a black and brown street,
the vein from which it issues

along the fog line,
her small talk naked,
pregnant as the pillow,

Niagara Falls of a movie
rushing into his eyes,
in which she is an actor

who hates to be attractive
on the pale television
since time is election

and so is money,
seamless as a lake
on a grey autumn day—

narrative as immersion,
the evaporating pages
of his dying history—

but he asked to be chosen
in the raw negotiation
love turned out to be;

she on the other hand
is all skill and nerve,
the egg in an illusion

beneath collapsing hats
as the night lies in bed
like a selfish new wife,

the perilous question
always in pain, a thin
smile on its vacant face,

and the heart is
a construction surprised
by each containment,

wintry as amazement,
language as knowledge
when grandfathers topple

and happiness is rich;
yet, stable in nature,
corners don't shake

and neither do reminders,
so she looks over his shoulder
into kinder buildings,

scratched to the limit
in a maze of corridors
where she removes her clothes,

relentless three flights up,
and they can do no wrong
in the crummy resurrection

constructed of their bones,
where a little love in back
is worth all the begging,

when the canary really sings
and the sea is just the sea
only in memory, glowing dully

under the moon, and the moon
itself is pure, the simplest
of concepts rattling in the sky,

yet they are not the ceiling
and they are not sleep
with its fears and shadows,

the average appalling day
celibate as the mind,
since the first and last

make their deep impression
and then nothing more,
and sun fills all the rooms.

The Explanation

the blank anthem pours
over the general public
and this is not the last
of my unhappy ideas

you can say mistake
a thousand times and mean it
may no one sign goodbye
no one sink and swim

in brilliant restlessness
or a taut state of rest
death is only love
staged like a mourning

a solitary christ
sweating in the heat
& at the luncheonette
the unnameable speaks

only the strange is true
and pleasure runs smoothly
yet the bride is priggish
albeit in the dark

the president of all things
is a neon figure walking
through paradisical forms
in the nausea of language

blue glass bottles
are an unfamiliar fact
life counts down
but I remain direction

gratuitous frock
in an unlocked room
and as the mind sags
the world grows more alert

the dairy queen weeps
a sudden misalignment
of character and act
circumstance's map   ·

in interest and in flood
we make the moderate strange
the ordinary range
from homocide to laundry

the household gods are small
and often in agreement
exalted one day
believable the next

the aria sings itself
in a well-lighted alley
and the angels who hear it
lift their eyes in cunning

malodorous fairies
their hands in cream
the phenomenal energy
of a hypocritical man

something is disguised
something is unmarked
at variance with the swimmer
and the riptide beneath

we watch the very stir
of nothing as it cleaves
to depth and weather
nothing goes away

you love an afternoon
of thematic revelation
a radiance that exists
at odds with the linens

one is free to be sick
of any kind of litter
broken statuary gods
the logic of a song

epiphany's name
is tiffany now
and the guests flirtatious
as has been the case

Private Lives

the ampleness of

being in white

birch forests hating

our children but

ordering burgers for

ninety-nine cents

in privacy and

in history would

not the moment

make nor nature

turn to gold

between and within

the discipline's limit

unless and until

in tourmaline grandeur

earthy and rehearsed

the day's equations

were at standstill

if we repeated

at freak speed

the unopened windows

fire engine momentum

against what leaning

cracked like wheat

mother is river

father is silk

lucidly a remnant

quick nocturnal beasts

twisted like forms

mindless and annoying

the smoothest children

repeating the known

beyond our hearing

a monster sings

incubus nihilist night

machine rapture reading

speechless at last

lacking utopic focus

prong's weak tea

a baffled statue

vapor and jargon

crimp and shine

star harp's edges

solid as blood

our formative years

perfect as numbers

along some line

all evidence scatters

a jittery picture

we are accomplished

singing and hinged

the lyric poem

river of rivers

waiting in wings

one dirge word

hat's old head

the hieroglyph banquet

a bloody divination

all doubt ripe

white cedar splendid

in luminary gloom

shall we dance

the gay expose

eyes tight shut

drowning not waving

on karaoke beds

early to yearn

nearly to lean

squeaky green field

dog and dish

infinity is sleepy

I'm feeling leaky

slippery when wet

Sartre looked shaken

in Cartesian kitchens

a secret drawer

morning's made man

the attic bird

head of steam

the fierce hymn

sung in science

and in mind

Sortes Evangelicae

childish silent
trust-fund seizure

regretfully lustfully
anatole albacore

lately flood-plain
early valley

needless frighting
opposable thumb

curved endured
quadrant staircase

scenery tracery
transvestite leaning

elite marine
niggardly sisters

ugly sunny
attraction window

discipline daughter
boned mobile

flabby tyrant
magic companion

heave strove
prove tooth

handsome doormat
idiot clusters

blue ambition
dissident hombre

instead penfold
alien context

virulent weegee
dedication crisis

fiery pamphlet
leaking season

initially partly
seemingly cheeses

ingenious teenager
dimensional freezings

revolting blessing
shining writing

extensive threshold
perilous marriage

albeit moreover
heroic however

generous crushing
amelia teaspoon

baxter capacity
passionate egress

helpless young
summoned photon

feverish stigma
infatuation luncheon

synapse answer
discourse conundrum

linoleum lightning
tympani ending

laden outline
infinite gesture

carillon comfort
tidy arrival

larkspur funfest
metaphysical shadow

Under Flood

The world is a problem
in its complicated armor.
What tender hands

of ghosts and beatings
cherished in prison,
what shining backs

of roaches in the black
nets of thought,
what inhabitants of

a summer fierce as life—
on a heart-rending
verandah, on a seismic chart,

on a daydream blossom,
on a nerve toy compass,
on the bright floors of science,

on seasons at the bottom,
on green ancestral birds
motionless as a stone,

naked as jars, disheveled
as laundry, black as a harvest,
pale with enactment,

fatal as a cane, impotent
as Venice, heavy as
a tavern. Prompt

in the mind, the actual
is flecked with blood
but likes a calm repose,

as if the act of being
were more akin to
reading. Lavish in

its candor, the real
accepts these words
for what they aren't.

Distance is stricken;
the season leans exactly;
we are under flood.

Internal as a shadow,
eternal as the earth
where gods will never go,

the wind whips cleanly,
the sun shines neatly,
and the cat is fat.

American Sphinx

As it arranges
space, the hooked
eye catches the

purest of contagions:
infantile brightness, like
stout or cream,

pockets of houses
turned out in
the cold, and

soldiers standing on
bridges starched as
shirts. To hold

them empty against
a new rib,
to pour ripe

eyes over flat
land is the
"long wet dream

with the hat
and the bags."
Up elation's stairs

in one hot
groove, original as
shade and bitter

to the root,
love's in ruins.
The soul of

a camera turns
in the dark,
a knife grows

hard, and still
one bleeds to
hear last words.

Arrested by the
language, we are
quaint with burdens.

The bedroom voice
is thick with
children. Raging and

sleeping, hands are
directions. *I will,
I will.* Against

green space, your
own face is
a "vague terrain

of time" shot
with a penny
camera. A woman's

safe hands, white
with scars, blur
to the bone.

Unforgiven

1

As dust falls in the clean house,
a woman pauses to listen
to a farther edge of summer.

She is event's horizon.
Infinity has no distance.
A cat stalks in the yard.

The sound of flesh being struck
is the sound of history.
A long shelf of water

on memory's speechless field.
A bird caught in the attic
beyond the ancient lake.

But always middle water,
as "A" in eye's relation.
She practices the having.

Felt in trance's branch,
leaves fall like fields
into the work of earth.

The thought is hard as play.
At the margin watch intently,
leaves excite the glass.

2

As television blinks
its fundamental truths
sincere as arctic ice,

memory of that future
happens like a life.
Yearning breaks in reason's space;

the eagerness of belief
goes crazy as an island.
This is thinking's gift:

to lie awake indifferent
beneath the beaten roof,
the swept path under a crow

flying straight as stone
to disappear in dark
greyer than its wing.

On rainy nights in doorways,
everything suffers autumn.
The sandstone lion wakes.

The slight weight of children
leans against a wall.
An old confusion stands

beyond limit's fog—
passion minus grace
on a summer of evenings.

3

Rising from its form,
instant as a tracing,
the song is an amalgam

of augury and blackbird,
imagination and habit.
Within that math, astonishing

islands. Raw mud huts
on plains and hills.
Days and days of rain.

In a bony sanitorium,
on a monkish sofa in
Anton's study, maturing

toward infinity but aging
past light, swallowing
ominous drinks and visiting

the zoo, the world occurs.
She drifts along with it,
monotony and chutzpah

fragrant as horizons.
Her blood runs cold
with sorrow & obligation.

So and thus. Thus and so.
Fa, mi, la, do. Occasion's
last knock signifying all.

Necessary Errand

After quiz shows fade
and the mind is silent,
after neutral acts

obscure yet fatal,
the blunt trauma object
shakes with pleasure.

The dream story's
violence has its own
faithless heroes,

rapid eye movements,
but nothing called
thought even as

procedure, just the rich
spasmodic gestures
of life on the run.

Thin as a threshold,
oblique as an act,
nobody fucking gets it

or gets it in the neck.
The allegorical weather,
with its aging rains

and latinate diction,
struggles to exist.
In the house of words,

the color of the yeti
against blown snow
is all that matters.

We are always clear
but rarely transparent.
The wedding cake bride

lives on sugar
in trailer park heaven.
A perilous journey

in quarter-note bursts.
A soft and serious father
gazing over water.

I think you get
my drift. The sharper
the errand, the more

your rhetoric fails,
"another spoiled quest"
for the grail to remainder.

Discovered in his attic
by a real estate agent,
mummified and

leaning in his chair,
an East German man,
dead for four years,

seems to watch
the ripe television,
which of course is on.

Printed in the United States
3484